Your Piggy Bank:
A Guide to Spending
& Saving for Kids!

MONEY
· · · · · · · FOR · · · · · · ·
FOOD

MARY ELIZABETH SALZMANN

Consulting Editor, Diane Craig,
M.A./Reading Specialist

Paula Austin, B.A. Elementary
Education/Math Consultant

visit us at www.abdopublishing.com

Published by Magic Wagon, a division of the ABDO Group,
8000 West 78th Street, Edina, Minnesota 55439.

Printed in the United States of America, North Mankato, Minnesota.
062010
092010

 This book contains at least 10% recycled materials.

Editor: Katherine Hengel
Content Developer: Nancy Tuminelly

Library of Congress Cataloging-in-Publication Data

Salzmann, Mary Elizabeth, 1968-
 Money for food / by Mary Elizabeth Salzmann.
    p. cm. -- (Your piggy bank: a guide to spending & saving for kids!)
 ISBN 978-1-61641-029-2
 1. Money--Juvenile literature. 2. Food--Costs--Juvenile literature. 3. Mathematics--Juvenile literature. I. Title.
 HG221.5.S264 2011
 332.024--dc22
                    2009053778

What About Tax?

Given the audience and nature of this series, we chose not to directly address taxes as an element of an item's price. For the purposes of this series, the taxes are included in the prices!

CONTENTS

COINS AND BILLS

PENNY		**ONE CENT**	1¢ or $0.01
NICKEL		**FIVE CENTS**	5¢ or $0.05
DIME		**TEN CENTS**	10¢ or $0.10
QUARTER		**TWENTY-FIVE CENTS**	25¢ or $0.25
DOLLAR BILL		**ONE DOLLAR** equal to one hundred cents	100¢ or $1.00

More Coins

There are also coins worth fifty cents and one dollar.

More Bills

Some bills are worth more than one dollar. Look for the number in the corners of a bill. That is how many dollars the bill is worth.

SPENDING MONEY

Here are some important ideas to think about when spending money.

Price
The price is how much you pay for something.

Quantity
The quantity is how many things you buy.

Quality
The quality of something is how well it is made or how well it works.

Value
Value is how price, quantity, and quality work together. It is good to think about value before you buy something.

Meet Adam!

Adam's parents give him money. He gets to decide what to buy. Follow along with Adam as he tries to make good decisions.

Adam's Goal

Adam wants to buy an ice cream sundae. It costs **$6.50**. His **goal** is to save enough money to buy the ice cream sundae.

Adam's Savings

Adam puts his savings in his piggy bank. He saves a little bit at a time. Small amounts can add up to a lot!

SNACK

Adam likes to get a snack at the community center. His parents give him some bills and coins. How much money did they give him?

Organize the bills and coins into groups. Then add the groups together.

Find the total of each group. Then add the group totals together.

COUNT THE BILLS

There is one dollar bill.
1 dollar equals $1.00

Write the total of the bills.

$1.00

Add the first two groups.

$1.00
+$2.00

$3.00

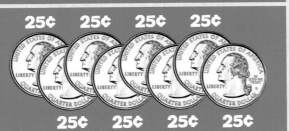

GROUP COINS TO MAKE DOLLARS

There are eight quarters.
8 quarters equal $2.00

Write the total of the coins grouped in dollars.

$2.00

The sum of the first two groups is **$3.00**.

COUNT THE REST OF THE COINS

There are three dimes.
3 dimes equal 30¢

There are four nickels.
4 nickels equal 20¢

There is one penny.
1 penny equals 1¢

Find the total.
30¢ + 20¢ + 1¢ = 51¢

Write the total of the rest of the coins.

Write it in dollars, not cents.

$0.51 is the same as 51¢.

$0.51

Add the coins to the sum of the first two groups.

$3.00
+$0.51

$3.51

The total amount of all the bills and coins is **$3.51**.

Add It Up!

Adam's parents gave him $3.51 to buy a snack. The community center **staff** gives each kid $1.00. Now how much money does Adam have?

> I did the math on a piece of paper. You can see how I did it below. The total is $4.51.

Do the Math

Adding decimal numbers is a lot like adding whole numbers.

Line up the decimal points.

$3.51
+$1.00
————

Start from the right and add each column.

$3.51
+$1.00
————
    1

Put a decimal point in the answer. It goes below the other decimal points.

$3.51
+$1.00
————
$4.51

Include the dollar sign in the answer.

Do the Math

Subtracting decimal numbers is a lot like subtracting whole numbers.

Line up the decimal points.

$4.51
- $2.50

Start from the right and subtract each column.

$4.51
- $2.50

1

Put a decimal point in the answer. It goes below the other decimal points.

$4.51
- $2.50

$2.01

Include the dollar sign in the answer.

Subtract It!

I can put $2.01 into my piggy bank! You can see how I figured it out at the top of the page.

Adam has $4.51 to buy a snack. A bag of pretzels and a bottle of water cost $2.50. How much money does Adam have left?

Adam had $4.51. He spent $2.50. Now he has $2.01. Adam puts the leftover money into his piggy bank.

WATER

9

Adam's Piggy Bank

$0.00
+$2.01

$2.01

DINNER

Adam's scout troop stops for dinner. Adam needs something to eat and drink. He can spend **$4.55** or less.

What should Adam have for dinner?

$3.00

$4.05

$4.25

$0.50

$1.60

$2.00

Do the Math

Some of the combinations cost more than **$4.55**. Let's look at a couple of examples.

$3.00 + $1.60 = $4.60

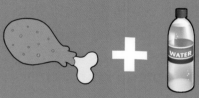

$4.25 + $2.00 = $6.25

Decision Time

Adam has two **options**. He can buy the taco with the milk. Or, he can buy the hamburger with the milk. All the other combinations cost too much.

$3.00 + $0.50 = **$3.50**

$4.05 + $0.50 = **$4.55**

If Adam buys the hamburger with the milk, he will spend all his money. If he buys the taco with the milk, he will still have some money left!

I'm going to have the taco and the milk. Then I can put **$1.05** into my piggy bank!

Adam had **$4.55**. He spent **$3.50**. Now he has **$1.05**. Adam puts the leftover money into his piggy bank.

11

Adam's Piggy Bank

$2.01
+$1.05
———
$3.06

Add It Up!

Adam wants to buy dessert. The apple pie costs **$2.70**. A scoop of ice cream costs **$0.50**. What is the total cost of Adam's dessert?

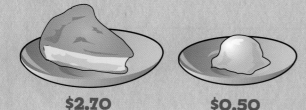

$2.70 $0.50

> I figured it out! It was easier when I wrote it down on paper. The total cost is $3.20.

Do the Math	Line up the decimal points.	Start from the right and add each column.	Regroup when digits in a column total ten or more.	Write the decimal point in the answer.
Adding decimal numbers is a lot like adding whole numbers.	$2.70 +$0.50	$2.70 +$0.50 ___ 0	1 $2.70 +$0.50 ___ 20	$2.70 +$0.50 ___ $3.20

Do the Math

Subtracting decimal numbers is a lot like subtracting whole numbers.

Line up the decimal points.	Start from the right and subtract each column.	Regroup as you would when subtracting whole numbers.	Write the decimal point in the answer.
$4.00 - $3.20 ――――――	$4.00 - $3.20 ――――― 0	3 10 $4̶.̶00 - $3.20 ――――― 80	$4.00 - $3.20 ――――― $0.80

Subtract It!

Adam's parents give him $4.00 to buy dessert. Adam knows that the total cost is $3.20. How much money will he have left?

Adam had $4.00. He spent $3.20. Now he has $.80. Adam puts the leftover money into his piggy bank.

> I can put $0.80 into my piggy bank! You can see how I figured it out at the top of the page.

Adam's Piggy Bank

$3.06
+$0.80
―――――
$3.86

LUNCH

Adam and his parents go to the farmers market. Adam needs fruit for lunch during the week. He can spend $4.00 or less.

Which fruit should Adam buy?

$2.75

$2.75

$2.75

Think About It

To get the best value, he needs to think about price and quantity.

PRICE

All of the boxes of fruit are the same price.

QUANTITY

The box of peaches has 15.
The box of apples has 7.
The box of bananas has 4.

Decision Time

Adam can afford any of the boxes of fruit. But he needs to make sure he has enough to last a week.

PEACHES

There are 15 peaches in a box. That is more fruit than the other boxes. But Adam can't eat that many peaches before they spoil.

BANANAS

There are 4 bananas in a box. That is less than the other boxes. Adam would not be able to have a piece of fruit each day with his lunch.

APPLES

There are 7 apples in a box. That is enough to have one for lunch every day.

The apples are the best value for Adam. He could get more peaches for the same price. But some of them would **spoil** before he could eat them. And four bananas just wouldn't be enough for the week.

I'm going to buy the apples. They're the best deal for me. I'll have enough fruit for the week. And no fruit will be wasted.

Adam had **$4.00**. He spent **$2.75**. Now he has **$1.25**. Adam puts the leftover money into his piggy bank.

Adam's Piggy Bank

$3.86
+$1.25
———
$5.11

TOO MANY PEACHES

Adam and Olivia both bought fruit for the week. Adam got seven apples, one for each day of the week. Olivia chose the peaches because she got more for the same price. But is buying more always the best choice? Let's see what happens!

Adam, look at this huge box of peaches I bought! There are 15 peaches in here! And it was the same price as the smaller boxes of fruit.

Wow, that's a lot of peaches, Olivia. But peaches don't stay fresh very long. Do you think you can eat them all before they go bad?

No problem! I love peaches. They are my favorite fruit!

It looks like Adam made the best decision. He ended up with the right amount of fruit!

BREAKFAST

Adam's friend David had a sleep-over birthday party. In the morning, they go out for breakfast. Adam can spend $3.75 or less. What should Adam have?

$1.00

$4.00

$2.00

Think About It

To get the best value, he needs to think about price and quality.

PRICE

The doughnut breakfast has the lowest price. The yogurt breakfast has the highest price.

QUALITY

Adam knows he should eat a healthy breakfast. The yogurt breakfast is very healthy. It has the best quality. The doughnut breakfast is the least healthy. So it has the worst quality.

Decision Time

Adam can afford any of the breakfasts. He thinks about each meal's price and quality.

THE DOUGHNUT

The doughnut breakfast has the lowest price. But it also has the worst quality. It would save Adam the most money. But it wouldn't be very good for him.

THE YOGURT

The yogurt breakfast has the best quality. But it also has the highest price. It would be healthy. But Adam would have to spend all his money.

THE CEREAL

The cereal breakfast doesn't cost a lot. And it is pretty healthy. It has a low price and good quality. He won't have to spend all his money, and he'll have a healthy breakfast.

The doughnut breakfast isn't healthy enough. Adam doesn't like its quality.

The yogurt breakfast is too expensive. Adam doesn't want to spend that much.

Adam thinks the cereal breakfast is healthy enough. And it doesn't cost a lot!

The cereal breakfast is the best value! It has a low price *and* good quality. I'm going to have the cereal. Then I'll have $1.75 to put in my piggy bank!

Adam had $3.75. He spent $2.00. Now he has $1.75. Adam puts the leftover money into his piggy bank.

Adam's Piggy Bank

$5.11
+$1.75
$6.86

WHO ATE A HEALTHY BREAKFAST?

Choosing the cheapest thing isn't always the best idea. Usually, the less something costs, the worse its quality is. Saving money might not be worth it if what you buy isn't good for you.

It looks like Adam chose a better breakfast than David. Adam's healthy breakfast gave him enough energy to win the race!

SAVING UP!

Adam's **goal** was to buy an ice cream sundae for **$6.50**. He saved a little bit of money at a time. Finally, he was able to buy the sundae! He is proud of himself for making good buying decisions.

Adam saved **$6.86**. He saved enough money to buy the ice cream sundae!

$6.86

$6.50

BEST VALUE

Remember that value is a combination of price, quantity, and quality. You usually can't have the best of all three. You have to decide which is most important. If you think about value, you will make good buying decisions.

USE COUPONS

Check the newspaper or the Internet. You might find **coupons** for **discounts** on food at stores and restaurants.

BUY IN BULK

Buying in bulk means buying a lot of something at once. You can often get a better price when you buy a large quantity.

SHOP AT FARMERS MARKETS

Farmers markets sell fruits and vegetables that were grown nearby. It is often fresher than what you can buy at a store.

GLOSSARY

coupon – a small note that offers a discount on a service or product.

discount – an amount taken off of the price of something.

goal – something you try to get or accomplish.

option – something you can choose.

organize – to arrange things in a certain way.

spoil – to become rotten or stale.

staff – the people who work at a place.